Making Love

The Conversation

A Novella by

Marie LaVerité

ISBN-13 978-0-9986060-3-3

ISBN-10   0-9986060-3-0

Deposited in the Library of Congress

First Edition.

Set in Times New Roman 12 point

Lexingford Publishing LLC

New York San Francisco Ottawa Hong Kong

www.lexingfordpublishingllc.com

Preface

Since leaving France at age 24 with my husband to earn my PhD in Psychology in the United States, I have been fascinated by a glaring but little-recognized difference in the sexual cultures of my birth country and my new home.

In France, young lovers tend to talk about every aspect of their romantic relationship—especially their sexual preferences and experiences—before launching the ship, so to speak. This seems particularly true in urban areas of France. In fact, it is has been said that the sidewalk café familiar from every French brochure would cease to exist were it not for the endless arguing, confessing, teasing, pouting and apologizing of young lovers over coffee. When romance fails to bloom, friends often say the couple "talked it to death."

In America, by contrast, would-be lovers seem to purposely avoid much knowledge about one another on their race to the bed. This absence of knowledge extends to ignorance about one another's family, job, friends, and even last name.

I have speculated for a year or two on how an American couple would survive the ordeal of French-style romantic interrogation—or, more accurately, pre-romantic interrogation. The fruit of my thinking took the form of this novella. It is, of course, neither a psychological or sociological treatise. Instead, it is a portrait—or a sketch for a portrait—of one conversation in the most familiar of American coffee houses, Starbucks.

I assure all readers, including my clientele, friends, and students, that I have not been eavesdropping on their private and personal conversations. My characters here are wholly fictional, as are the situations they discuss. At the same time, they are hardly alone in the issues they face in approaching serious love commitments—issues that draw as deeply on their mutual sense of humor as on their curiosity, common sense, and romantic desires.

I hope you enjoy preparing with Paul and Michele for their third date. I welcome your reaction through my publisher at www.lexingfordpublishing.com. Finally, I acknowledge Starbucks as the registered trademark name of Starbucks Coffee Company.

Marie LaVerité, PhD
New York, New York
May 10, 2017

Table of Contents

Chapter One

Starbucks

Michelle glances at her watch as she reaches for the door to enter Starbucks. Right on time—9:30 am. A good thing or would it be better to be a little late? Well, she is here. And she beat the rain storm just starting to spatter the sidewalk. Michele pushes back her shoulder-length auburn hair, unconsciously smoothes out her camel slacks, and looks over and around the Starbucks crowd for Paul. The crowd seems to notice her as well. She is, in a word, lovely.

"Hi, Michele. Over here." Paul, slim and sporting a new crew-neck sweater for the occasion, gives a wave over the crowd. On an ordinary Saturday he would still be in sweatpants and a old t-shirt after his daily run. This isn't an ordinary Saturday.

"A table at the back at Starbucks on a Saturday morning. You must know someone."

Paul shakes his head. "Nope. It was sitting here empty. What are you having?"

"Grande latte, nonfat milk. You?"

"I already ordered. Chai soy latte, no water."
She laughs. "That sounds like a dessert, Paul."

"It's sweet, I'll admit." Paul makes a stir stick stand up in his cup. "And thick."

Paul returns to the table with her latte. "So here we are."

"Here we are." They both smile. Silence.

Michele breaks the ice. "You said we needed to talk. That sounds like the beginning of a 'you're-a-nice-girl-but' goodbye."

"No, no. Absolutely no. Just the opposite. I—"

She waits.

"I want to talk about—you know, our dates, the future." He glances away to the rain pelting the coffee shop windows.

"Our dates? Both of them?"

Paul puts his face in his hands, then smiles sheepishly at Michele. "This is all starting wrong. I really liked our dates—'both of them,' like you said."

She smiles and gives an exaggerated exhale. "Whew! Well, I did too. So there."

Their eyes meet. He reaches across and takes her hand. "I am so, so terrible at this."

"This what?" She really doesn't know.

"Let me just talk—obviously my strong suit!" He takes a long sip of his chai. She crosses her arms in a mock haruumph and nods for him to go for it.

"First date was kind of checking each other out, right? You obviously chose a public place in case I turned out to be a creeper."

"Which you are not," Michele interjects. "I have checked that box: Paul is not a creeper."

He smiles. Short silence. "Then our second date."

"Yes, our post check-out date. Fun movie, great dinner. Nice kiss."

"Very nice kiss."

"Standing on my doorstep. Lovely, lovely kiss. And then we said goodnight."

"But we were close, right?"

"Close?"

"Close to the door opening and you leading me inside."

"Yep, I must admit. It crossed my mind."

"But it was only our second date," Paul concedes.

"And my roommate was home."

"You didn't mention that. Now I feel better."

She unfolds her arms and puts both hands on the table. He puts his hands on top of hers.

"What this is all about," he begins, then starts over. "What we need to talk about is date number three."

"I would love to," she whispers. "When do you want to pick me up?" He laughs.

"So," he says, "I'm 28 and you're, what, 26?"

"You remembered," she says. "But you don't know my birthday."

"And continuing my thought," he says, walking his fingers across the tops of her hands, "you as a young but precocious and extremely desirable woman know how third dates tend to go."

She wags her finger. "Not always. I have been in several third date situations over my many, many years of living that went nowhere. Nada. And my roommate wasn't home those times."

"I am proud of you." He gives her a little salute. "But let's stick with our third date."

"Yes, let's." She leans forward.

"So we go to a concert or a play—something nice--who knows, a tractor-pull.   And then after a wonderful evening we end up at your doorstep again. And your roommate isn't home."

"No, she isn't. In fact, she's gone for the entire night."

"And." He pauses. "It is possible—I'm not saying inevitable—but possible, or maybe probable, that we move to the next level."

"As in shopping for a condo on a higher floor?" She's teasing. "Possible? Probable? Inevitable? I guess we won't know until the moment."

He looks into her eyes and doesn't blink. "Won't we?"

"Are you asking me now?"

"Just your opinion. Your best prediction."

"My best prediction . . . " She stirs what's left of her latte and studies his face. "Swami says, 'Very likely couple make love.'"

"That's what my swami told me, too." He plays with her finger-tips. "But . . ."

"But?"

"Here's the thing: do we really want it to be the movie thing where they rip off each other's clothes, buttons are popping everywhere, a bra gets torn in half—"

"I'm having a hot flash." Michele fans herself dramatically. "And I'm going to wear an old bra."

"But you do get my point, right?"

"You mean that movie sex is over before you can finish a mouthful of popcorn?"

"Exactly. Popcorn sex." They laugh. She looks over her shoulder to see if others are listening. They're not.

"My hot flash is over. You were saying?"

"I'm 28 and you're 26 . . ."

"Yeah, I got that part."

"And I think we're mature enough to talk."

"About date three."

"About date three."

"Especially the way the evening ends?"

"That would be the precise part we could talk about." He moves their cups to the side of the table as if preparing to arm wrestle.

"So let's say—" Michele chooses her words carefully— "let's say that we make love on that mystical, romantic, roommate-absent third date. You want to—" she knits her brow—"like, talk about it now?"

"I do."

"Here?" She glances around the coffee shop.

"I think so."

"Wouldn't you rather just let it happen—I mean, hypothetically, possibly, what you said."

"I want to talk about it because," he says with emphasis, and then drops his voice. "Because I really, really"—he decides not to stick in a few more really's—"like you. I don't want popcorn sex."

"It sounds different, doesn't it. Sex. Love making. Sex. Love making. Which do you prefer, sir?"

"I'll take love making anytime. But it doesn't happen by accident."

"You mean we're fated for one another?"

"That sounds fine to me. But what I really meant was that strikingly 'together' and, in your case, gorgeous people don't just let it happen."

"You, Paul, are a planner. That's exactly what a planner would say."

"In fact, I'm not a planner. Most of the dumbest moments of my life happened when I didn't plan. Which is most of the time."

"But this time it's different?"

"With you, I want it to be different." He kisses her hand and she smiles.

"Is this where I get out my steno pad and we write a love making script?" She's confused about where he's headed.

"No. I would forget my lines anyway. And you would have to put chalklines on the floor—on the bed—so I could hit my marks."

"But you do want to talk about 'it,' is that right?" Michele waits to understand.

Paul blurts out, "Now I'm getting the hot flash. I don't get off on talking in a coffee shop about making love."

"So we talk because . . .?" The question hangs in the air for a long moment.

"Because I care about what works for you. What you like, what you don't."

Michele cleared her throat. "This is the most serious Starbucks conversation I've ever had in my life."

"I'm glad I'm your first—Starbucks' most serious conversationalist. Maybe they will write that on my cup."

"So if I'm game, and that's a big if—IF I'm game for this serious conversation, how exactly does it work? Do we take turns revealing our most private impulses and turn-on's and turn-off's and—"

Paul interrupts, "That would be weird, I admit. Your turn, my turn. That sounds a little juvenile, like Truth or Dare."

"And remember, we are, as you like to point out, 28 and 26."

"That we are."

Chapter Two

Gambit

"So answer my question, seriously. How does this work?"

Paul scoots back in his chair. "I haven't the faintest idea. I guess we just—talk . . . and see where it goes."

"I'll go with a couple probationary tries." Michele makes a funny face. "But if I start feeling like an eel is climbing up my leg I swear to God I'm going to clam up. I will also tell my roommate she's staying home forever."

"Deal."

"So this was your idea. You start."

"Oh God. The popcorn is smelling better and better." Paul makes a fake groan. "But OK. I'll start."

"You'll start." Michele thumps her fist on the table like a judge.

"Remember what you said about sex and love making?" Paul feels like he is losing his voice.

"I recall you saying something about sex and love making," Michele replies.

"Well, what do you think about the words 'love making'? I mean, we haven't actually used the 'L' word together—I mean, not yet."

"Not after two dates."

"Certainly not. Inadvisable." Paul smiles. "But think about it. Are we 'making' something—you know, literally 'making love' by having sex?"

Michele looks puzzled. "Philosophy 101, which I failed. Are we manufacturing some emotions that we don't really feel—I mean, yet? After two dates."

"Yeah, that's what I'm getting at. I don't mind at all calling it 'love making' if that's what's happening. But to me, 'making love' is way, way more caring and considerate of the other person than just sex."

"You're saying sex can be good but . . . "

"Good but different than creating love emotions—lasting stuff."

Michele puts a finger to her forehead. "Something tells me there's a very important story about to be told." She whispers, "You can trust me. I won't tell anyone at the gym or the nail salon."

She makes Paul laugh. "OK," he admits, "there's a story, and all parties referred to shall remain anonymous FOREVER. Besides, you don't know her."

"For about six months, back when I was unforgivably young at 24, I dated a girl—woman—she was 24, too—and we quickly fell into this rhythm of working all week and having sex, maybe or maybe not, on weekends. But that's definitely what it was, at least for me. Sex.

"Sometimes I would look at her when she was sleeping and say to myself, 'Wow, I'm having sex with a good-looking woman.' And then in my imagination I'm eighty. I die and they write on my tombstone, 'He had sex with a good-looking woman. More than once.'"

Michele stops him. "And the sex wasn't good?"

Paul pauses. "We're telling the truth now, right? The sex felt good at the time but didn't feel good in the morning, if you know what I mean. We were together physically and then we went back to our own worlds."

"Did you live together?"

"It was crazy. I kept some of my stuff at her place and she kept some of her stuff—in fact, a ton of her stuff—at my place. We sort of lived between two apartments. So the technical answer is, 'No, we didn't live together.'"

"Did she love you?"

"That also was nutsoid. She would say things like, 'You're the kind of guy I could fall in love with' and I would blurt out 'me, too.' Until I realized how ridiculous that sounded. I think I would have stumbled into using the 'love' word if I asked her to marry me, but it never even came close to that."

"So how does the story end?"

"I had to go away on a business trip for a couple weeks. On my way back, I called her from the airport to say that we needed to take a break."

Paul took a breath and continued. "So picture this: the phone rings and she says, 'Paul, I think we need to take a break.' She beat me to it. But I'm sure neither of us shed a tear. It had just gotten old. Our hearts weren't in it and we knew it."

"Did you talk to her about things?"

"Nope. We never talked again, and I heard she took a job out-of-state a few months after we broke it off."

"So, Paul, what do we learn from this most interesting story? What is the teachable moment?" Michele puts her fingertips together like a professor.

"Hmm. Dunce that I am about love—I mean, sex—I would say that, at the very mature age now of 28 I have learned that I don't want a string of casual encounters, even if they last six months. Did I get it right?"

"You tell me. So sex is risky for you because you worry that it's not going to lead to anything meaningful and satisfying?"

"That question is so horribly, cruelly intelligent that I'm not going to answer it. But I will say that after two dates, I know whether a relationship is headed toward sex or toward making love. We decided those were different, right?"

"Very."

"And we've had two dates."

"And?"

"Don't take this the wrong way: I don't want to have sex with you. I mean, of course I do, but if we could kind of think of it as making love it would really help me out."

"But we're not ready to use the 'L' word, is that right?"

"I think you will feel a little funny about it after two dates. That's a big word to lay on the table."

"And you wouldn't feel funny?"

"Yeah. I don't want to scare you away."

"Good answer." Michele crosses her arms again. "So you think we should talk things through?"

Paul nods. "I think it is a good idea. I also think we may end up laughing at this whole attempt and I will feel like an idiot."

"That's possible . . . or probable . . . or inevitable. Kind of like making love on the third date."

Paul gives her a helpless look.

"How about those Yankees!" she says breezily.

"OK, this is my last, best try and then we shop for popcorn. Can you imagine a couple who know each other really well? They're deeply in love. When they make love they don't have to fake anything or ask questions. They know each other's signals. Pleasing the other person in bed is pleasing themselves."

Michele agrees. "I think if we looked all over the earth we might find such a couple. Not my parents, for sure."

"Mine either." Paul tries to pick up the thread. "But imagine such a couple. How did they get there? I don't think it was just years and years of time with one another. At some point I think they opened up and just talked about making love. You know, what worked for them and what didn't so much."

"Maybe they talked at a Starbucks." Michele squints her eyes.

"And maybe the guy was starting to sweat," Paul replies.

"No, no. Don't sweat. You have me interested in this couple. Maybe we should double-date with them for our third date. They sound fascinating."

"Ah, yes, the couple. So they live happily ever after because making love works so well for them. Other reasons too. But they are kind of inside each other's minds when they make love. They don't worry about making the right move or the wrong move. They are like a perfect ballet or something."

"Making love in a tutu. One or both of us?" Michele gives a coy, innocent look.

Paul smiles back and holds up his hands. "You win. This is an impossible conversation to have between a man and a woman. Making love from this day forth shall remain a mystery not to be discussed between us. It will happen or not, and buttons and ripped clothing will fly everywhere. Possibly."

Michele sighs. "Then it will be over and we say?"

"We will say something innocuous like, 'That was great' and 'Was it good for you?'

"And we will both say 'yes, it was nice' even if it wasn't very good and 'yes, it was fabulous' if it was pretty good, and 'oh my God' if we are still catching our breath." Paul pursues the thought. "But what will we be thinking? That's the part I don't get. Maybe you will be thinking 'he's kind of selfish in bed' or I'll be thinking 'I hope to God that was OK for her.'"

"A conundrum. How to avoid a train wreck, or a slight derailment, or a train arriving late—or too early—on our third date. And we don't want to miss the train, do we?"

"No. I for one do not want miss the train. And how did we start talking about trains?"

Michele frowns. "I thought it was clever, especially that part about the train being late or too early. That's kind of talking about making love, isn't it?"

Paul concurs. "It's a start. You've got me worried about the train arriving too early part. I don't think that's my problem, but third date love-making—trains move pretty fast."

"Terribly fast. They can shred a perfectly good bra."

"And that's not good." Paul phrases it as a question.

"Well, it's good in a way, especially in the movies. But you're right—it's not as good as it could be."

Paul gives a little 'high five' in the air to no one in particular. "We are definitely on the same track, and I'm not talking about the damn train. 'As good as it could be.' That's what I thought we could talk about."

Michele is thinking. "Well, we've made a little progress. Arriving early in love-making is kind of disappointing. Agreed?"

Paul warms. "Yes. Point number one: Paul will not arrive early."

Michele puts her hand over her heart. "Subpoint number one: Michele will not arrive early." She rubs a blush away from her cheeks and says quietly, "But will she arrive late?"

Paul whispers back, "I am willing to wait as long as it takes. Hours. 'Til morning if necessary. I don't want you to worry about arriving late."

Michele looks at him steadily. "That's a bit of a relief. Women worry about not making it happen fast enough. Men worry about making it happen too fast."

Paul murmurs, "OMG, we're talking about making love. We're actually making progress."

"All the way to Point One, which I can't exactly recall. But it was something about relaxing about when the stupid train arrives." Michele pretends to be confused.

Paul says, "Clarification: the stupid, lovely, long-awaited, and much desired train."

Michele puts her chin into her hand and leans forward. "If this gets more obscure, I'm going to have to get a double latte to keep up. I surrender all attempts at being clever or shy. Talk and I will listen. If you're lucky, I may say something once in a while."

Paul runs his finger around the lip of his cup. "I will talk—in short bursts—like this—and then shut up—to see—if—if—you want to say anything. OK?"

Michele mouths a very slow "O----K----."

Chapter Three

Clothing

" Let's retrace our hypothetical steps on our mythical—but highly probable—third date. We've had a nice evening doing something fun. We're back on your porch and I'm not kissing you goodnight because that didn't work out so well on the second date. We're not at my apartment because it's being painted. You open your apartment door and, behold, there is no roommate present. In fact, she has left a note saying 'Gone for the weekend. We need milk.' You give me the note to frame."

Michele twirls her finger in the air. "Go on."

"We recall our long, torturous conversation about popcorn, and therefore I do not follow my strong impulse to begin undressing you on the spot. By the way, how do you feel about the undressing thing? This might turn out to be Point Number Two."

"I'm glad you asked and I do have something to say. When I undress I have a chance to check all my bits and pieces. If we've been bowling or roller-skating or horseback-riding or, who knows, even dancing, I may want to see if I reek. That's the problem with having you undress me. So mark it down. The movies be damned, this woman prefers to undress herself, preferably in private."

Paul pretends to be writing on a note pad with his finger. "Duly noted. Self-undressing but not a sign of lack of interest in making love. Very good reasons provided."

"By the way," Michele inserts, "my habits about undressing don't have to be yours. It would be a bit strange if we each retreat to a separate room to undress and say, 'See you in the bedroom in a few minutes.' That's pretty Victorian."

"Another point well-taken." Paul continues to 'write:' - 'Paul may undress at will because he is less conscious of his bodily state, even though he is prone to sweat during tense moments in Michele's presence.'

"So where does that leave us?" Michele pretends to remember nothing.

"Well, I suppose you could say, 'Would you like something to drink?'"

"And you would reply?"

"I would definitely say, 'No thanks. I'm fine.' I mean, we've had two or three drinks on our date already that evening. I'm avoiding what too much alcohol does to men's sexual performance."

"Ah, sexual performance." Michele pronounces the phrase like a therapist. "Not love-making performance? But never mind. I must confess that another glass or wine or two for many women may cause that insufferable train to be delayed. Catch my drift?"

"Caught and noted. 'Go easy on the alcohol once in the apartment. Again, very good reasons given, although in metaphor."

"So I repeat: where does that leave us?"

"I think you have undressed in some hidden nook of your apartment, checked everything you want to check, showered if necessary, and come out. A question: Are you wearing something or . . . ?"

"Definitely something. Sheer and quite appealing, but something. And you?"

"Being a man's man, I am sitting on the couch having not taken off anything. I am staring at a copy of *Vogue* I picked up off your coffee table, but I am not thinking about the magazine at all. I am, as they say, in anticipation."

"In anticipation while fully dressed. At some point that must become uncomfortable. Again, you catch my drift, right?"

"I do. And the point is recorded: Paul cannot remain in his clothing while Michele, sheer and appealing, is standing before him. His clothing is not that large."

"So?"

"So I do not scatter my pants, shirt, socks, shoes, and underwear all over your living room, as I might in my own apartment. This is when I embrace you and kind of waltz you toward the bedroom. That's where I quickly get my clothes off. Although I haven't timed myself, I predict that you will be impressed with how quickly I get my clothes off in this hypothetical circumstance."

"I see. Well, in fact I don't see. You no doubt still have your briefs on. Is that true?"

"You've read my mind. I'm not one to be the first to jump into the pool totally nude. After all, you've still got your sheer and appealing thing on."

"Remind me to buy that before our third date."

"Gladly."

Paul continues. "So we fall or slither or climb or tumble into the bed still partially clothed?"

Michele nods. "We do. That's comfortable for me. How about you?"

"Yes." Paul starts then stops. "You're going to ask me why."

"Of course. Why?"

"An erect male—and trust me, I will be an erect male at this point—can look a little like a towel rack just standing there. The underwear is a temporary but necessary transition."

"My God, a towel rack!" Michele shoots Paul a wide-eyed expression.

"Don't have false expectations. Towel racks can be for bath towels or hand towels or wash cloths. Without boring you with statistics, I would expect something along the lines of a hand towel rack of medium dimensions. Sturdy, though. Oh yes, sturdy and dependable."

Michele half-giggles. "And still gift-wrapped in underwear. I'm getting quite the picture."

"So now we're in bed and embracing. Lights on or off?"

Michele ponders. "I suppose this is one of those binary decisions. We can't have it both ways. I vote for leaving the bathroom light on, which casts a pleasant glow across the bedroom."

"And I second the motion. Glaring lights can make a person feel on stage," Paul adds, "with all the dangers of stage jitters, especially on a third date. But who knows? By date five or six, we may revisit this vote."

"We may. Are you talking about turning off all the lights?" Michele mentally reviews the switches in her apartment.

"Not necessarily," Paul responds. "I'm talking about turning off some of the lights."

Michele purses her lips. "Turning on all the lights may be down the road a piece. Maybe dates seven or eight."

"I think I suggested dates five or six. But I don't want you to be uncomfortable."

Michele fans herself. "I feel like I'm in a sun-tanning bed right now. Is it hot in here or is it just me? You talk for a while. I'll just nod if I agree and say 'Hell no' if I don't."

Chapter Four

Sheets

"We left off in bed, but it was undecided whether covers of any kind were part of the scene. Believe it or not, I'm thinking we climb under the sheets."

"Why the 'believe it or not'?"

"Because guys have the reputation for having sex, which we have wisely re-defined as making love, on the kitchen counter, the floor, the road beside their Harley, that sort of thing. I personally like to climb under sheets, especially because I'm substantially more exposed than you are. Cold is the enemy of towel racks."

"That's right. I'm still wearing my sheer and appealing yet-to-be-purchased negligee. Does the word 'negligee' make you uncomfortable?"

"I think my mother had a negligee and every woman her age had one as well. Or two or three. Let's just not call it a negligee. Don't they call it 'something comfortable' in the movies?"

"They do." Michele touches her fingertips to her chin. "So I can imagine myself saying, "Wait while I slip into something comfortable.' But when we're in bed, am I really going to say, "Can you help me off with this something comfortable? That sounds uncomfortable."

Paul thinks for a moment. "You're right, you're right. Let's just say this.: 'Paul, help me off with this.' That will communicate the message without raising any thoughts about my mother."

"Perfect."

"Perfect. So the code word is 'this,' not 'something comfortable.' Did you express your opinion about under or over the sheets?"

Michele responds, "No. But I do agree. I'm a sheet-lover too. They can always disappear later, but at first its cozy to pull something over us, don't you think?"

Paul unbuttons the top button of his shirt. "You're right. It's hot in here. Glad we're not covered with sheets right now."

"But on the third date, remember the cold. The towel bar thing. Sheets are a good thing. Or I can turn up the thermostat in my apartment."

"Marked down and recorded. We're under the sheets by common agreement. And now—"

"Wait a minute," Michele winces. "A horrible thought crosses my mind and I'm sure yours at the same time."

"Trust me, no horrible thought will be crossing my mind." Paul crosses his heart.

"Yes it will as soon as I whisper it in your ear."

"Whisper it now and we'll see what happens."

Michele leans forward and murmurs, "Do you have any sexually-transmitted diseases?"

"Oh God," Paul moans. "The towel bar just fell off the wall. It broke into tiny, tiny pieces. But wait—" He reaches into his wallet.

"What's that?" Michele scoots closer.

"The newest wrinkle for what they euphemistically call 'sexually active young adults'—a credit-card-sized certification from, ta-da, a licensed physician seen within the last two weeks bearing scientific—scienTIFic— evidence that I have 'none of the above,' including AIDS, herpes, syphilis, or any other coitus interrupter. What do you think of that?" With a flair, he passes the card across the table to her. She reads it with arched eyebrows.

"I wish you hadn't called it a credit card," she answers. "I mean, cash left on the bedside table is one thing, but ringing this all up as a credit card transaction is, well, a little gauche. Even though my credit rating is good. Very, very good."

"It's made of paper," Paul points out. "No credit card is made of paper. I will never call it a credit card again. Or a frequent flyer card. Or a passport. Just forget all those words. I wish I hadn't said them. The point is a doctor— a DOCTOR—certified that I am sexually healthy."

"I'm starting to relax." Michele pushes her chair back a little. "But half the horrible thought is still crawling around us like a bed-bug."

"What's that?"

"I don't have a card, so you don't know about me."

Paul scratches an eyebrow. "Can I just take my chances? I don't think women tend to carry these cards. Maybe they are for men only."

"But," Michele breaks in, "I bring this to the table." She slaps a stapled couple of computer pages on the table. "My annual lab report," she explains, "done no more than ONE week ago, certifying by LABORATORY evidence—a scientific LABORATORY—that I too am sexually healthy. I pose no danger to you, except, of course, stealing your soul and condemning you to a lifelong monogamous relationship"

Paul grins. "And the horrible thought has now exited the bed?"

"It has. Presuming we are faithful to one another between now and our third date. A third party for either of us could rob us of science and all its assurances. I am positive that I will not be romantically involved with anyone else before our third date. Can you say the same? No pressure intended."

"None taken. I agree completely. No interlopers before our third date. Besides, this card"—he waves it between them—"cost me $200, and that's just my co-pay. I'm sure your laboratory report was equally expensive. We don't want to pull the rug from under science at these prices."

"So $200 is your price for remaining faithful?"

"You misunderstand. I would remain faithful for a dollar."

"A dollar?"

Paul tries to explain. "I mean that no amount of money would tempt me to undermine our third date."

"You will remain faithful for free?"

"Or $200, whichever you prefer. Just mark me down as faithful."

Michele won't let it drop. "The reason being that you don't want to miss the opportunity—and a grand opportunity it is, I assure you—to go to bed with me. Or might there also be a hint of emotion involved?"

"Of course. Emotions galore. I could be more specific, but at this point I thought the 'L' word might be a bit heavy and premature before our third date.'

"The 'L' word as in 'love'? 'I will be faithful because I'm falling in love with you?'"

"That is precisely the word I was thinking of. Mind you, I'm not at all afraid of the word. I just don't want to say it prematurely and scare you away."

"We already know how we feel about premature."

"Indeed we do. We don't like it."

"But at the right time . . . "

"Yes, that's it. At the right time, the word will be, well, lovely."

"And welcome."

"Of course, a person under the influence of passion might murmur, 'You are so incredibly lovable' or 'God, you are so lovely.'"

"But those are both different than whispering 'I love you.'"

Paul waxes philosophical. "Unfortunately, that's true. We can say 'I love this Starbucks' but we feel awkward for the time being blurting out 'I love you.' Weird, isn't it?"

"Weird, but all part of our sexual culture. You can't go around declaring love for everyone you date."

"Nope. But at the right moment with the right person-- "

"Enough said. I think we are in complete agreement."

"Lovely. So to speak."

"Do you remember talking in general terms about the towel bar? It must have been ten minutes ago." Michele taps the dial on her watch.

"Ah, yes, the towel bar. No problem. Repaired entirely. Back on the wall. Perhaps even larger and sturdier than before, having certain anxieties lifted from it."

"Anxieties regarding certain words leading to other words like 'proposal' and 'til death do us part?'" Michele asks.

"I think so. Those words are perfect, but at the right time."

"Probably not the third date."

"Probably not. Do you agree?"

"I do. But I suppose that phrase also may sound premature. Women can't say 'I do' without thinking twice."

Paul sets his palms on the table and takes a deep breath. "Well, we have wrestled the obstacle of faithfulness to the ground, wouldn't you say?"

"What a relief," Michele breathes.

Chapter Five

Briefs

"Don't say 'relief,' please. That word is synonymous with the train arriving too early. We're under the sheets. You are still wearing 'this,' formerly known as the artist 'something comfortable.' And I am still in my briefs. By the way, I have never used the word 'briefs' to describe my underwear. I have never heard any man say that word."

Michele puzzles. "What do you call them? Underpanties? Undies? Tidy whities?"

"You don't know as much as you think you know," Paul objects. "Men who don't buy bikini underwear—and I am among that vast, vast group—buy either boxers or tighter, white underwear that cannot speak its name. I don't know exactly what they are called. White underwear, I think. But in any case, I only wear boxers. That is what I wear and that is what you can expect to see, or half-see in the dim light from the bathroom."

"Are they plain or do they have a humorous theme? You know, little frogs or candy stripes on them?"

"Why do you ask?" Paul pretends to be defensive.

"I need to know whether I am expected to take notice. If they do have little hearts or polka-dots or barbells or something on them, I wouldn't want to just ignore a thing like that. How would it make you feel?"

"Well, in the moment it would make me feel awful if you were thinking about polka-dots on my boxers. If you want to know the truth—and that's what this conversation is about, right?—some of my boxer shorts do have, well, patterns of things on them. My mother gave me a four-pack featuring holiday themes. But BELIEVE ME when I tell you that I will not be wearing any of those on the night of our third date. My boxer shorts will be plain tan or blue, with absolutely nothing for you to notice. So there."

"I've got to get another latte. Do you want another chai?"

Michele stands up. Paul says 'no thanks' to the offer. He watches her find her place in the short line. He can feel his heart slowing for the first time since the conversation began. 'She's going to talk about the weather when she comes back to the table,' he tells himself. 'Just when we're under the sheets all the rest is going to go silent. She probably thinks I am the stupidest man on earth.'

Michele returns with her latte. "Is this chair taken?" she asks.

"No," Paul smiles. "Please sit down."

"Oh, no, I'm sorry," Michele teases. "I just wanted the chair to join my girlfriends over there." She motions over her shoulder, then sits down with her second steaming latte. She rests her chin on her hands and looks at Paul with doe-like eyes. "It's getting cloudy outside. Maybe rain."

'The weather,' Paul thinks to himself. 'We're on the verge of solving Newton's Third Date paradox and I push her into talking about the weather.'

"So, where were we?"

Paul brightens. Perhaps all is not lost.

"You're going to be up all night," Paul says.

Michele lets her chin slip from her hands. "Bragging? That's a big leap from just getting under the sheets." She looks down and tastes her latte. "Up all night. My."

"No, I meant the caffeine." Paul mentally gives her points for being far quicker on her feet than he is. "Ah, yes, I do recall. The warm and embracing sheets. Healthy, scientifically certified people nestled beneath them. That's where we were."

"I feel like the orchestra has just played the prelude," Michele says. "Is the action about to begin?"

"No, that's the surprising thing," Paul says lightly. "We fall asleep almost instantly. I tend toward narcolepsy. How about you?"

"You told me I was going to be up all night. Promises, promises."

"OK, I'm being deadly serious now. I think I took a huge chance trying to have this kind of conversation for the first time in my life with someone I really care about. But if you want to stop now and just enjoy your latte, I'm fine with that. In fact, in my imagination right now I'm resting comfortably in my nondescript boxers under extremely comfortable sheets next to a goddess wearing nothing but 'this.' So I'm a happy guy. Do you really want to talk about the weather?"

"No," Michele says with conviction. "I think we should see this thing through. We've slogged through fields of mud and bitter rain and dead comrades all around. We've climbed in and out of the trenches and all is not quiet on the Western front. We're not going to give up now that we've reached the front lines. You with me, soldier?"

Paul gives a little salute, encouraged by her energy. That caffeine is working.

"So, to sum up, we're presumably—I don't say 'certainly' or 'inevitably'—in each other's arms at this point. I think we can trust hands—" he holds his up toward her for inspection—"to do their work. Hands have a life of their own."

"Mine are getting you out of those boring, unillustrated boxer shorts." Michele smiles.

"And mine are wriggling you out of 'this'." Paul pantomimes a complicated slipping of 'this' up and over Michele's head.

"And now," Michele says a bit triumphantly, "we are finally as God made us. How long did this all take?"

"Apparently an eternity," Paul answers. "From the time we walked into your apartment, we're probably past fifteen minutes or so. But those are moments well-spent. That ain't popcorn sex. We're taking our time."

"I think you are right," Michele responds nonchallantly. "We haven't jumped on the tracks to see if the train is coming. We busied ourselves like proper passengers until it arrives."

"I can't even hear the whistle yet," Paul interjects. "And I swear on my mother's negligee that's the last time I will refer to TRAINS. By the way—" Paul stands up, "I need one of those lattes you're drinking. Be right back."

Michele watches Paul take his place in line, this time a longer queue. She thinks, for about five seconds, on the vagaries of life that would make one man in that line so important to her. She realizes she is staring and turns to her purse, really just a little tote bag. 'Playing with my purse is stupid,' she says half-aloud to herself. She resolves to just sit, Zen-like, and wait for Paul's return.

"Whew!" he exhales when he finally sits down again. "That was a barista adventure.' Along with his latte he brings an oatmeal cookie the size of a small dinner plate. "I was going to get two, but look at the size of this thing." He elevated it like the Sacred Host. "Big enough to feed a horse."

Michele gives a mock "neigh" and Paul realizes what he has said.

"No, I'm the horse. You're not the horse." He sighs. "I'm an ass."

Michele reaches over and breaks off a piece of cookie. "Trigger is ready for her oats."

Paul perks up. "You know Trigger? I thought that was something grandfathers experienced, fathers heard about, and we young-un's didn't know about at all."

"Actually," Michele says, with a long pause for effect, "I have seen the actual Trigger, now stuffed for all to admire in some roadside museum in Southern California. I was fourteen and we were on one of those drive-forever family vacations. I actually petted the stuffed Trigger. This very hand. Haven't washed it since."

"That's incredible," Paul mumbles through a mouthful of raisin oatmeal. "And did you see Dale Evans?"

"I saw her life-size wax double but I don't believe she was stuffed," Michele says. "I was afraid to touch her. Do you know that she started the craze of naming girls Dale?"

"Again, incredible." Paul is watching more than listening. He likes the way she plays.

"Yes. Girls were named Gale prior to the heyday of Dale Evans. In fact, even after parents named their girls Dale, people would ask 'Is it Gale with a 'G'? 'No,' young ladies would answer in one voice, 'it's Dale with a 'D' as in 'David.'"

"And then the Dale craze kind of petered out?" Paul asks.

"I think it was the stuffing thing—and I'm not really sure about that. But I wouldn't name my daughter . . . our daughter . . ." she felt herself flushing ". . . any hypothetical but not inevitable daughter Dale if it brought to mind anything stuffed."

"But it did set the pattern for syllables in good names. First name one syllable, last name two syllables. So it is written, so let it be." Paul can play too.

"Give me an example."

"Bob Costas. Tom Brokaw. Pam Shriver. Jane Goodall. Those are solid names that roll off the tongue. Dale Evans. No wonder we're still talking about her."

"And Roy Rogers. I see what you mean."

"And Love Making."

"What?"

"One syllable, two syllables. Memorable, interesting, extremely powerful." Paul is proud of bringing the conversation back around.

"It does have a better ring than two syllables, then one final syllable, like 'having sex' or 'getting laid.'"

"Bite your tongue," Paul hushes, handing her another chunk of cookie. "What would Dale Evans say? 'I got laid by Roy Rogers last night'? I don't think so."

Both smile and let a long moment of silence fall.

Chapter Six

Work

"So we are back to work on our conversation, is that it?" Michele flips back her hair and looks Paul in the eye.

"We are back to work, and for a noble cause," Paul answers. "The problem is I can't quite remember where we quit work."

"It's hazy to me as well," Michele fakes. "I seem to remember something about sheets."

"Ah, sheets. It's all coming back to me now." Paul obviously had used his time standing in line to figure out how to move the conversation forward.

"So we're between the sheets," Michele says bluntly. "But wouldn't it be better to leave everything after that as a surprise? A new adventure? Kind of like taking your first blimp ride and having no idea what it will be like?"

Paul thinks about Michele's attempt at checkmate. "Surprises are fine—unless you've booked your blimp passage on the Hindenberg. Then everything goes down in flames just because we were afraid to ask the pilot, 'Is there any chance this thing will explode?'"

"Let me get this straight." Michele leans forward again. "We're going to talk about love making, one syllable, two syllables, in excruciating detail out of an abundance of caution so that we don't crash and burn?"

"I think that's prudent, don't you?"

Michele considers for a moment. "Here's what I think, buster." Michele makes little mock fists. "If your abundance-of-caution conversation—sorry, *our* conversation--takes the flavor of a game of never-have-I-ever I'm out, even if you have plied me with oats."

Paul looks shocked. "That's putting the cart way before the horse—let me rephrase—that's not any gentleman's question of a lady."

"Or," Michele inserts, "any lady's question of a gentleman."

"I frankly don't give a fig about your sexual history," Paul says archly. "That was what Adam said to Eve."

"I thought it was an apple, not a fig. And Eve had no sexual history, did she?"

"No, it was a fig. But I still don't care about it."

"Adam and Eve just let things evolve," Michele presses on. "I don't think they did a lot of romantic planning. Did they know enough words to have a conversation?"

Paul shrugs. "I worry about their children, though. Those pages about the mates of Adam and Eve's children got ripped out of our family Bible, I think."

"But it gives us a starting place for awkward topics," Michele responds. "And the answer, sir, is that 'No, I have never slept with my brother.'"

"Do you have a brother?"

"No, but that's not the point."

"We're more alike than different," Paul soothes. "I have never slept with my brother, except in a tent with four other Boy Scouts, and I do in fact have a brother."

"And those are exactly the kind of questions we're not going to ask, right?" Michele wants ground rules.

"We've put incest entirely off the table." Paul wipes away the crumbs left from the cookie. "This is going to be an entirely above-board, though under-the-sheets, conversation from this point on. Comfortable and non-intrusive. Nothing that will make either of us squirm."

"Good," Michele answers, settling in.

"Good," Paul repeats with finality. "So we left things with mutual hands doing God's work in helping us out of our remaining clothing. Are we agreed?"

"We are."

"And there are no special preferences or requests at this juncture?"

"None. I can't get out of my something comfortable without dislocating a shoulder. You're welcome to help."

"Ditto for under-shorts, or whatever." Paul is still struggling for the word.

"And no doubt we are embracing, if only because one sheet doesn't exactly provide a lot of protection from the cold. I will be sure to turn my thermostat up. My roommate usually keeps the apartment about 68 degrees, no matter what I say."

"But we're forgetting about the roommate, right? She is GONE and not coming back for hours, many hours. We are not talking about sleeping with brothers real or imagined and we are definitely not thinking about your roommate returning unexpectedly. Some thoughts have to be out of bounds."

Michele picks up the thread. "OK, so we're nude and embracing. Let me ask you your own question: Any special requests, requirements, expectations, scenarios, imagined situations, or fantasy-life projections that you would like to bring up at this juncture? I mean, just to ruin the moment?"

Paul doesn't miss a beat. "Nope. I am content to be embracing you and kissing your lovely lips. In fact, I am ecstatic at the prospect."

"How easily expectations creep in," Michele muses. "In your mind, we are obviously face-to-face, correct? We're not in cuddling position?"

"If you want to be in cuddling position, I can kiss the back of your neck," Paul says gallantly.

"No, I'm fine with face-to-face. Cuddling is what they call a red herring—something thrown in to see if you're being careful about your assumptions."

"Au contraire," Paul objects. "The details are as follows: I have wrapped you tightly against me with one arm and have my remaining hand, the one on my other arm, of course, gently cupping your breast. Our legs are suitable intertwined. Enough detail, sister?"

"Eyes open or shut?"

"How bright is the light from the bathroom?"

"Why does that matter?"

"If it is pitch black in your bedroom I suspect that I will not have my eyes open. That would be like opening an empty refrigerator."

"It would?"

"The more you think about it, the more the light bulb will come on for you."

"From the refrigerator?"

"No, from the bathroom, which we agreed would be our glowing source of illumination. Or have you mentally turned off all the lights at this point?"

"Not at all. I want to see if your eyes are open. It's an important thing to me."

"In other words, an expectation or special request at this juncture?"

"Well, doesn't it make sense that we look at each other at the beginning of love making? If you close your eyes, I may worry that you're thinking of Dale Evans or Pam Shriver or any number of one syllable, two syllable women from your sordid past."

"One of my great regrets in life, just so you know," Paul says, "is that my past was not nearly sordid enough. Not by a country mile."

"I could say the same thing," Michele responds, "but I don't want to suggest that my past was just sordid enough for my liking. We agreed to avoid those awkward never-have-I-ever questions. I trust in the great scheme of things we both have pretty admirable permanent records, if I do say so myself. B+ to A-, only a couple tardies."

"We must have gone to the same school," Paul agrees. "That was my exact record as well."

"And the eyes?" Michele reminds him.

"Definitely open as long as there is something to see. Closed and not thinking of Dale Evans or Trigger or anything remotely stuffed if there is nothing to see in the dark."

"I think I can assure you," Michele says, with an alluring hint, "that you will have something to see."

Chapter Seven

Strategy

P aul is caught without words for a moment. He can't say, 'And you'll get an eyeful, too' without sounding like a braggart. His voice cracks a bit: "That will be nice. Very nice."

"And I notice that you've moved quickly along to only one breast. I have two, just to be clear. What are your intentions with the one breast you are cupping? I'm quite attached to it."

"I don't have a clear breast strategy, but I think I can say without equivocation that I will cup it with the utmost loving care, verging on adoration, and—"

"Verging?"

"OK, in absolute adoration without any verging. The cupping, of course, can't last forever. I'm not a living bra."

"So the cupping is in progressive motion somehow? Would you conceive of this motion as upward or downward?"

Paul pretends to think for a second, although he knows his answer in advance. "I think I speak for every red-blooded man, very few of whom you have slept with, in saying that you don't climb a mountain without the intention of standing gloriously at the top."

Michele knits her forehead. "How might that be translated into English? I just want to be ready with my icepick and crampons."

"Put simply, the gentlest, most adoring cupping of the breast soon—very soon---ascends to the nipple."

"I worry, Paul, that you continue to use the singular when referring to breast attention. Just as I have two breasts, I have two nipples. I am getting the distinct idea that one nipple is about to get enormous attention while the other is flapping in the wind, so to speak, maybe even outside the sheets."

"That's because you have forgotten about my one arm still embracing you. I'll get to the other nipple in good time, I assure you, but dual nipple attention at this early, early stage of making love would require me to lie apart from you or on top of you, then reach over with both hands—anyway, as appealing as this may turn out to be at a later stage, I don't think it sounds, well, adept early on. Do you?"

"You're entirely right. In this case. By the way, Paul, do you realize that some men in this Starbucks are carrying in their wallets a card listing the 100 highest mountains in Northern America?"

"So?"

"That's not your expectation, is it? The highest peaks? Climbing above the treeline into some mammary Himalayas, the peaks of which vaguely resemble the Hindenberg with nipples about the size of the former polar icecap?"

"Not at all. In fact, I relish more moderate-size mountains, even hillocks."

Michele seems appeased. "Think West Virginia. Lovely rolling hills. Mountain mama. Take me home. That sort of thing."

"Noted and appreciated."

"That's a relief in a way. Some insecure women, myself obviously not included, worry that their breasts will be somehow disappointing in a first love-making situation. I know that is silly."

"You have absolutely nothing to worry about."

Michele gives a mock frown. "I know I have nothing to worry about. I was concerned about all those insecure women I was mentioning."

"Oh yes, them."

"While we're in the neighborhood of expectations, are you Jewish?"

"No, but I could be. Is that important to you?"

"I'm getting at the somewhat delicate issue of the natural or altered state of the male organ. Why do they call it an organ?"

"You're right. It's not a kidney or a pancreas. Those are organs. This is more like a feature. They should call it the male feature."

"And your male feature is . . . ?"

"Oh, circumcision! I didn't see where you were headed. There's a pun there somewhere, but not worth mentioning. Yes, I am, if that matters to you."

"It doesn't really. I'm just not one for surprises if they can be avoided. Besides, a minute ago my nipples—at least one of them--were front and center. You should not be embarrassed to talk about your male feature."

"Indeed I am not."

"Well, are you proud to do so?"

"Now that would be silly. I am neutral. Neither proud nor ashamed. Think West Virginia, as you said, not the Washington Monument. I'm not one of those guys who has a list of the 100 highest peaks in North America. I don't even think about them. This is getting hard, isn't it?"

"Pardon me?" Michele suppresses a giggle.

"This discussion. I thought we could just compare notes, finish a latte or two, and set a time for our third date. But I realize now that there's a lot to talk about."

"What about your nipples, Paul? Do they get hard when you're aroused?"

"I honestly don't know."

"So your nipples are the Undiscovered Country for you. Imagine that at 28."

"I'm just not conscious of my nipples. Have you heard the expression, 'Useless as tits on a bear?'"

"I have not and please don't explain it."

"But you're very aware of your nipples, right? Especially when aroused."

"I am. They get hard."

"That's very nice for you—that's very nice for both of us."

"But don't set your cap quite yet. It's not something I control, short of an ice cube. And you said the refrigerator was empty. I mean, don't be disappointed if a nipple doesn't instantly come to attention. It doesn't mean that it's sleeping."

"One nipple can come to attention and not the other? The female body is quite amazing."

"If you figure out a way to free your other hand from the Spock death-grip you're embracing me in, I'm confident both nipples will cooperate."

"And that's a nice feeling for you?"

"A very nice feeling. Worthy of a kiss." She leans far over and kisses Paul lightly and quickly.

"That was nice."

"Worthy of several kisses, Paul. I'm trying to tell you something."

"Ah, I get it. Of course. Cupping and fondling and kissing. You have my word, and my word is my bond."

"But you have to also keep in mind, amidst your madcap fascination with my breasts, that I'm a girl who really,

really likes to kiss. Make-out kissing. Smooches. French kissing."

"You really like to kiss. Of course you do. I do too."

"Do you want me to write it on your hand?" She reaches for her purse. "This is not something we want to forget in the midst of nipple mania."

"No, I can remember. 'Kiss the woman. She really likes to be kissed.' Got it."

"Otherwise, it might seem mechanical. Me looking away at the turned-off night light, you pursuing your conquest of my breasts. What does that sound like?"

"Foreplay?"

"You are playing?"

"Certainly not. I am, what can I say, earnest and completely with the program at this point."

"Then why do they call it play? It sounds like the pinch-and-giggle pages out of an old French novel. The man chasing the woman around the bed. Really." Michele sniffs.

"That sounds exhausting and entirely unnecessary," Paul agrees. "Play is the wrong word."

"And I suppose 'fore' is short for 'before.' Something you do 'before' intercourse. But still part of making love."

"I believe you are right again. Love making includes foreplay. An average couple could not say 'we engaged in foreplay but there was no love-making.'"

Michele follows up quickly. "And we are hardly an average couple. Foreplay is underrated, don't you agree?"

Paul thinks about the question. "I hate to betray my gender, but I must: men tend to underrate foreplay in their eagerness for intercourse. You have hit upon a profound truth."

"I'm not concerned about men in general. I had you in mind. Do you want me to write it on your other hand? The one you haven't been using because it is going to sleep in an effort to hold me in a one-arm embrace?"

"No, I can remember. Foreplay isn't really 'fore' since it's wholly a part of love-making and isn't 'play' because, well, just because. The whole concept is very fresh in my mind, thank you."

Chapter Eight

Seriously

Michele pursues. "So we're not playing. But what are we doing? Being serious isn't quite the right phrase either. We're not working at the carwash, right?"

"Of course not. We're being semi-serious. I mean, we are making love. We've agreed that is no light thing."

"That's what I can tell my mother? He's semi-serious about me, especially in bed?"

"No, no. I'm entirely serious about you. But when we're making love, I'm saying that we're . . . we're . . . what's the word?"

"Having fun?"

Paul thinks for a moment. "Hmm. How does that word 'fun' strike you?"

Michele shakes her head. "Not very well. Fun sounds like throwing lawn darts with my nieces. I would say enjoying ourselves. Well, in truth we're not only enjoying ourselves. We're enjoying each other at the same time that we're enjoying ourselves."

Paul captures the idea. "Thomas Jefferson could not have said it better. At some point—God knows not today or tomorrow or next week or next month—we really have to write this down. It's a constitution for lovers. 'We the lovers in order to form a more perfect union . . . '"

"Get me back to the moment, Paul. Lovely, lovely kissing. By the way, my lips—" she touches her bottom lip with a finger—"my lips are definite erogenous zones. Just sipping this cup I've had two orgasms while we've been talking."

"You're kidding."

"I'm kidding. But not about the importance of kissing. Men forget about the Joy of Kissing. That cookbook was definitely written by a woman."

"Give me your pen. I'm writing this on my hand."

"No. Just say the title over and over to yourself. "Joy of Kissing, Joy of Kissing." Ink on your hands will smear, especially if your hands are moist. I don't want to end up as the girl with the marker-pen tattoo. That movie was already made."

"Some of that stuff doesn't wash off."

"Speaking of which—and this is leaping way ahead, I realize—what about washing? Can you picture us taking a shower together after making love?"
"I can picture it in theory, but how big is your shower?"

"Why do you ask?"

"If it's tiny like some apartment showers are, through no fault of their own, we may end up feeling like monkeys in a barrel."

"What?"

"You know, bodies half freezing because the other person is getting all the hot water and saying 'do you want me to wash your back?' when I can't even find your back in the mish-mash of body parts. It might not be a problem, but it could be."

"My shower is large. Do you want to take a shower after making love?'

"Put me down as a strong 'yes.'"

"Your reservation is confirmed. I like to take showers. It's refreshing."

"But we're not talking about jumping into the shower immediately after making love, are we? Have you heard the phrase, 'post coital lassitude?'"

"Yes, and it always has the word 'man' attached to it. Women never feel so energized as after making love. Leaping tall buildings at a single bound, cleaning out the empty refrigerator, rearranging heavy furniture, that sort of thing."

"I just want my Andy Warhol fifteen minutes of hibernation. There is no thought more excruciating to a man than jumping into a semi-serious shower immediately after making love. I—just—want—to— doze—off—for—a—few—minutes." Paul lets his head fall dramatically to the table.

"Then bring an egg-timer. Fifteen minutes of zoning out for you is right at the edge of unfortunate-but-acceptable for me. But that shower is taking place. It's romantic and it's important to me. I will shake you if you lie there like a lump for more than fifteen minutes after we're done."

Paul repeats morosely. "After we're done. That has such a sad sound to it."

"Well, don't chop your chickens too soon. 'Done' means 'OMG, that was incredible making love with you. I'm completely spent. Whew and gasp. Besides, men have a bad reputation for 'being done' before women are. And I'm talking about men in general, men out of books, men as I've heard tell. We're not going back to that 'Have you ever . . . ' business."

"You mean male orgasm. One and done?"

"I've heard—just heard—that can be a problem with some couples, especially if the woman in the highly hypothetical couple has the somewhat rare gift of finding herself multi-orgasmic in the right circumstances."

"Well, polish my boots. Multi-orgasmic. I could manage that if you have about four hours to spare."

"I'm not blaming you. I'm just saying that it's a male thing—again, so I've been told—to plummet from the height of passion to a snoring puddle within ten seconds or so. Icarus flying so high he touched the sun and took the basement elevator directly down to Snooze Land."

"Whereas the sun keeps on shining hot and bright for a while, is that the idea?"

"That's the idea. Eventually the sun sets, but it has been a very warm summer afternoon and evening, splendor in the grass, glory in the flower, all that Wordsworth stuff."

"Multi-orgasmic. I'm impressed."

"I didn't say multi-, multi-, multi- orgasmic. I just pointed out a potential difference in typical men and atypical women."

"I've got the message. I won't rush you to the end of love-making and you won't drag me prematurely out of the wonderful after-glow moments of post coital lassitude into the shower. Fifteen-minutes-at the max, then I will voluntarily stumble into a shower where I will feel myself going down the drain along with the scented soap suds."

"Deal."

"Deal."

Paul pushes his empty cup to the side. "I do believe we have resolved some of the pregnant questions regarding our third date. And I take back the word 'pregnant.'"

"I'm on the pill."

"Wonderful."

"You said some of the questions. Do you think we kind of glided over some items of mutual importance?"

"Well, if we did, let's certainly talk about them now. We'll never get a table like this again at Starbucks. What did you have in mind?"

Chapter Nine

Items

"These are hard issues to just hit on the head like a nail. The guy sitting behind me seems like he's getting increasingly interested in what we're saying." Michele motions behind her.

Paul looks over. "He's not. Right now he's doing a crossword puzzle. Before that he was looking for Pokemon for half an hour on his phone."

"And you've been able to observe all this while supposedly listening to what I've been saying?"

"I've been trained by the Agency to instantly notice everything and everyone in my environment. Isn't that the kind of thing that makes young women swoon?"

"If I ever swoon in your presence, please don't take it as a compliment. Take me to the ER."

"Anyway, you're entirely in the Trust and Safety Zone for whatever you want to talk about. I've got a couple things too, now that I think about it."

"Well, I should hope so. You started this conversation down an interesting but potentially thorny path and I'm just trying to keep up without getting scratched."

"Items, items. What are they?"

Michele holds up a finger. "We need to complete the canvas on what was erroneously called foreplay and is now known as enjoying ourselves and each other. There was the avid, enthusiastic kissing part that you've promised to remember. I'm still offering to write it on your hand. Just two words: 'Kiss her,' and I'll write very small."

"I thought we covered the kissing part. No need to write it on my hand. I'm sensitive to the high importance of kissing."

"All over?"

"Your body?"

"No, the wallpaper in my bedroom. Of course my body! Are you trying to make this difficult for me? You want to make me blush."

"No, I am definitely not trying to cause you any discomfort, although it was a fact in the 1800s that slave brides who blushed at the seraglio auctions fetched a higher price than those who didn't."

"Paul, what a stupid bit of trivia. And probably recorded by a male historian."

"You're right. The seraglio be damned. Of course I will enthusiastically kiss you everywhere you like to be kissed."

"Do you feel you have an adequate understanding of the clitoris?"

Paul pounced on the word. "We are virtual soul-mates. Peas from the same pod."

"All I will say is for me kissing there works very, very well. French kissing."

"You have been trusting to be so clear about your desires. Consider it my pleasure to comply."

"And mine. Now let's not talk about that anymore. The light has turned green and it's time to move on. Speed if you want to."

"No, no. I'm glad we didn't run that stop-light."

"You said you thought of a couple things."

"Well, yes. You're familiar with the male feature, otherwise known as the penis?"

"I am."

"No elaboration necessary. I would worry if you said 'no' to that question. Here's the thing: in the same way that you have an affection for being kissed all over, shall we say, I too enjoy a moderate degree of oral love-making. Focusing on me as the recipient of your attention, if you're following."

"I'm following. But you said 'moderate.' That's a rare word in the male sexual vocabulary. What are you telling me?"

"Just that in my case a little attention goes a long way. You don't need an egg-timer. Without dwelling unduly on fellatio, which has always sounded like Al Capone's hat to me, let's say that the duration of time spent in this aspect of love-making can be less or more, depending on your male partner."

"And in your case?"

"I tend to follow the Bauhaus principle: 'Less is more.'"

"Most interesting. And, by the way, entirely fine by me. What you have been describing so well has never been my favorite part of what was erroneously known as foreplay. You put it just right: a little goes a long way."

"Thanks for understanding. It just isn't one of my prolonged pleasures. I don't know why."

"You don't have to know why. This conversation isn't about knowing why. It's about what, what, what. It we don't know what, how can we possibly know when or where or how?"

"Which leaves us where?"

"Sperm. If sperm were the delicacy some people hold it out to be, it would be in the Deli section at Whole Foods. I choose not to satisfy my need for protein by sperm. I'm not criticizing the many, many sperm-lovers throughout the world. But just for myself, I'm not among them. In the right place at the right time, sperm is lovely. But that's about three feet away from where some men want to deposit it."

"I will take that to heart and definitely bear it in mind."

"Bearing it in mind is what you might say right after 'Oops, there.' This is one that I definitely think we should write on your hand. Or elsewhere."

"No, it's not necessary. I make you an absolute promise on this one. It's not my thing either."

"Ingesting sperm?"

"Yes. I mean, no. I am unacquainted with ingesting sperm. We were talking about making a deposit in the wrong bank—wrong, that is, for us, not for everyone. God bless the world's lovers wherever they wish to save. But I will not deposit sperm where it isn't welcome."

Michele exhales. "Thank God we got through that so delicately. We really are mature adults."

"I began to wonder when you came right out with the clitoris topic."

"I needed to. Making love without an orgasm just feels a little like running a 10-K and not crossing the finish line. No cheering. No heavenly collapse. Just 'I quit.' And the clitoris is the key to the kingdom when it comes to crossing the finish line."

"I know that."

"You know that but God apparently didn't. He or She missed the mark by about an inch or more in designing the female vagina. I guess it's redundant to say the 'female' vagina. Who else would have one?"

"How do you mean 'missed the mark'?"

"This is just a personal opinion, based on no special studies and funded by no Federal grant. But I think— remember, this is just me thinking—I think that men expect women to reach orgasm within a few minutes of, what shall we say, 'entry'. They don't realize that the clitoris is just a spectator to entry. 'Hey, I'm up here,' it's saying. 'Don't forget about me. Hey, I'm talking to you!'"

"Now that I think about it, you're entirely right. Men tend to assume that penetration is the end-all and be-all of sexual pleasure for the woman. But the male feature often does not adequately touch the clitoris during what, in the language of science, is called coitus."

Michele wrinkles her nose. "I hate that word 'coitus.' It reminds me of the name of a drapery cleaner. 'You have a lifetime guarantee when you trust your drapes and carpets to Coitus. In fact, we have a 40 percent off sale right now.'"

"Then let's just say 'intercourse.' That's a pretty tame name, right? In fact, there's a town in the Amish Country of Pennsylvania called Intercourse. It's about eight miles from Blue Balls. I'm not making this up."

"And I bet it's about 600 miles away from the little village of Clitoris. But let's stick to the topic. If straight-forward intercourse doesn't sufficiently arouse the clitoris, whatever are we going to do?" Michele gives a pout. "Whatever are we going to do?" Another pout.

Making Love: The Conversation

Chapter Ten

Good Vibrations

"There's kissing all over your body," Paul suggests.

"That is a good suggestion, Paul, and it may well work. But let's review: you're fully engaged from the waist down in whatever position you have in mind in the enterprise of intercourse. And somehow you are going to be kissing me in a way that leads to orgasm? No one has a neck that long or flexible."

"I see what you mean. Let me remind you of the American physician George Taylor, who in 1869 invented the steam-powered vibrator, which he patented under the name 'The Manipulator.' The more familiar electromagnetic version didn't come out until years later, invented by Joseph Mortimer Granville. I don't think he had a pet name for his invention. But it made him a millionaire."

"And he deserved every dollar. They both did, although I can't wrap my mind around a steam-powered vibrator." Michele gave a little shiver.

Paul presses her. "But certainly there's no embarrassment here, is there? Haven't vibrators in relationships become as common as KY lotion?"

"We've been out on two very lovely dates, but I'm not entirely sure I want to disclose much about one or more vibrators that may or may not be in the bottom drawer of my night table, under the nighties. That's pretty private stuff."

"But it does the job, right? Believe me, a lot of men are equally grateful for the vibrator—the electric one, which doesn't steam up the room or puff like a locomotive. Even though men don't usually own a vibrator of their own or carry one along on dates (or so I've been told by *Men's Health* magazine), they aren't exactly dashed when, sweaty with a pulse over 140, they hear their woman murmur, 'Let's try this.' A switch flicks on, the clitoris sings the Hallelujah Chorus, and all ends happily with a Great Amen."

"I appreciate the history lesson. If I had a vibrator, which is total speculation at this point, I would name it Mortimer in honor of its inventor. Can you imagine me whispering at the most intimate of moments, 'Let's let Mortimer help us'?"

"The idea is fine with me," Paul clears his throat, "and please don't interpret any laughter about the Mortimer name as disrespect. In fact, I would be willing to bring backup batteries or an extension cord for the hypothetical, possibly non-existent vibrator in your bottom drawer that might assist us in the pre-, during-, and post-intercourse involvement."

"You're a virtual MacGiver. Ready to rescue a damsel in her moment of need."

"I don't think we tip-toed through much there, did we? I notice that we're feeling more free to do away with metaphors and just say what we mean. I think that's very appealing about you."

"And you."

"It's as if we're trying to pour fine wine into a decanter without spilling a drop and our hands are getting more and more steady."

"Not a metaphor in sight."

Chapter Eleven

Metaphor

"Unless we happen to need one." Paul looks up to gauge Michelle's reaction. "A metaphor, I mean."

Michele is confused. "I thought we trusted one another just to come out with it, so to speak. You said the word 'penis' out loud in Starbucks and I said 'clitoris' more than once over my lattes. How liberal is that? Have you ever overheard that kind of non-metaphor-laden conversation in a Starbucks before? No, you haven't. We are breaking new ground. And now you want to retreat to needless smokescreens to talk about whatever else might or might not happen in bed?"

"Yep."

"If you must," she murmurs. "What's your metaphor?"

"It's more of parable—a heavenly story with an earthly meaning, as the radio preachers always say. It goes like this. When she was 22, Anne Milbanke married George Gordon, Lord Byron. The marriage somehow lasted two years before their final separation and divorce in 1816. During that time he savagely sodomized her, leaving her with rectal injuries that would plague her the rest of her life."

"What a horrible story. Is it true?" Michele makes a face.

"Unfortunately, yes. And I tell this gruesome story because—"

"You don't have to say another word. No way, on land, sea, water, or a waterbed. That is not an option for me. It's not on the menu."

"Good. That's how I feel too." Paul makes the Scout's Honor sign with his fingers.

"But that's just us," Michele cautions.

"Agreed. Others can do what they want. The heart wants what the heart wants. It's not wrong. It's just not our thing."

"Well said."

Paul leans forward. "Stories about Lord Byron come in handy at the most unexpected moments. He kept a bear in his University dorm room."

"Which is your way of saying, let me see, you aren't into cross-species sexual encounters?"

"No," Paul chuckles. "I was just telling you about Byron and his bear. He also kept a girl dressed as a boy in his room."

"Meaning?"

"Meaning nothing. Just another Byron story."

Michele scoots her chair back a little. "I don't want to hear about Byron when we're in bed."

"Not even 'She walks in beauty, like the night of cloudless climes and starry skies . . .'" Paul knows the famous poem by heart.

"I'll make an exception for that kind of Byron and try to forget about the rest," Michele allows.

Paul lets silence fall for a moment. "Isn't it easier to have this conversation now rather than at the height of passion in bed?"

"The height of passion. Are you sure you're not free-climbing the Matterhorn in your imagination? Keep thinking of the rolling hills of West Virginia. They will set you straight." Michele raises her pointer finger.

"I could have said depth of passion. All I meant was it's hard to make sentences or make sense when you're making love."

"I think you're right. You don't stop to debate the finer points in the moment. By the way, what's your take on talking during love-making?"

Michele replies, "As opposed to silence?"

"No. Talking of the sensual variety. Love talk. Sex talk."

"Well, here's another story." Paul rubs his hands.

"God, not Byron again," Michele groans.

"Unfortunately, yes."

"Lord. Go on."

"He liked love talk. He wrote the lines about 'she walks in beauty' after falling desperately, suddenly into lust or love."

"While making love to his wife?"

"Not exactly, or even approximately. He saw another man's wife at a party on June 11, 1814, and was so overcome by her beauty that he went home, got drunk, and then sobered up the next day to write his famous poem."

"But he didn't make love to her."

"No. He was busy sodomizing his wife and having incest with his sister, Augusta Leigh. But don't let that distract you."

"So your point about love talk?"

"Just that it doesn't have to be sex talk. It can be love talk. Or sexy love talk. Whatever."

"I'm not a prude," Michele interrupts. "But feeling that I'm somehow obligated to say a bunch of sex-coaching words to turn the other person on just isn't my thing."

"Not that it's wrong for others," Paul interjects.

"No. Again, God bless the others. Let them whisper or scream whatever they want to."

"Yep. Screamers and dreamers. I would rather be a dreamer."

"Besides, a lot of sex talk is so funny. It would make me laugh out loud to say something during love-making about my 'pussy.' Can you imagine if you saw a cat's head down there? You would be out of bed and out the window. Someone way back when must have liked cats a whole lot to paste them onto the female anatomy."

"I think maybe his name was Dick. That sort of got pasted onto the male anatomy."

"So we're resolved: all cat references and nicknames for Richard stay out of the sheets."

"But they aren't wrong."

"No. Fine for all the good folks who get their motors revving by talking sex slang. It just doesn't work for us by common agreement."

"So we will consider it out unless it naturally creeps in."

Michele raises an eyebrow. "Creeps in like a pussy? You dick."

They both laugh.

Chapter Twelve

Numbers

"Let's see, what haven't we covered—besides our naked selves? Completely out of curiosity and nothing more, what is your opinion of threesomes?"

"My opinion is that I have a queen-sized bed. I also have a queen-sized sexual sensibility. I wouldn't say "never," just "never for the next seventy years. I might feel differently when I'm ninety something."

"Agreed without reservation, even if you had a king-sized bed. Besides, a three-some to a man usually means two women. To a woman I suppose it means two men."

"Why don't we talk a little louder so everyone in this Starbucks can take part in our little survey?" Michele puts her finger across her lips.

Paul mouths a silent "sorry" and pretends to zip his lips.

Michele giggles at his sudden embarrassment. She whispers back, "How do you feel about pornography?"

Paul wrinkles his brow. "Grasshopper, you have asked a deep question to which I will give you a shallow answer. I think men are more visual in their sexual appetites than are women. Steamy romance novels don't have pictures, but I've been told they light the fire of exponentially more women than men. True?"

"That's probably true. Women are good at imagining. So your answer about pornography is . . .?"

Paul thinks for a moment. "I wouldn't bring it anywhere it didn't belong. And I get the strong sense that the Internet-type porn aimed mostly at men doesn't belong in a bed we share."

"That's pretty accurate," Michele answers. "I would feel kind of marginalized if you were staring at some porn flick when I was right there beside you, ready for romance. And you would feel odd if I were flipping the pages of some crotch novel while you were making love to me, wouldn't you?"

"I'm sure I would."

"So this is one more aspect of love-making that might be great for others but not for us. Do you think we are being too puritanical?"

"Not at all. Methodist, maybe, or even Unitarian, but not Puritans. We can let go and also let live. But back way, way up for a second. Doesn't it feel kind of good to talk about making love before accidentally making either of us feel awkward or pressured in the moment?"

"Let me take my pulse." Michele puts her thumb on her wrist. "About 80. That means that I am feeling something significant but not anxiety. So, yes. This conversation has been good."

"That other couple has been eyeing our table for the last ten minutes. Do you think we should give it to them?"

"Yes, unless you want to plan out our fourth, fifth, and sixth dates. That should only take a few days." Michele starts to gather her cup and napkin from the table.

"I think after the third date we're in free-fall," Paul replies with a hint of seriousness. "We jump out of the plane together and open a whole new adventure. Maybe for a lifetime."

Michele too becomes more serious. "Do you talk through this stuff with all your dates?" She wants him to say "no." She needs that answer.

"Just you," Paul says quietly and intensely. "It matters with you. It matters a lot."

'Good answer,' Michele thinks to herself as she rises from the table. She feels herself falling into something new, exciting, yet comfortable. Paul reaches for her hand as they leave Starbucks.

"You feel warm," he remarks, gently squeezing her hand.

"Caffeine," she smiles. "What else?"